Veteran Firemens Assocition

Souvenir of the Transcontinental Excursion from New York

to San Francisco

September 1887

Veteran Firemens Assocition

Souvenir of the Transcontinental Excursion from New York to San Francisco
September 1887

ISBN/EAN: 9783744661768

Printed in Europe, USA, Canada, Australia, Japan

Cover: Foto ©ninafisch / pixelio.de

More available books at **www.hansebooks.com**

VETERAN FIREMEN'S ASSOCIATION

OF THE CITY OF NEW YORK

→SOUVENIR←

OF THE

TRANSCONTINENTAL EXCURSION

FROM

NEW YORK TO SAN FRANCISCO,

SEPTEMBER, 1887.

*ALSO CONDENSED HISTORY OF IMPORTANT EVENTS IN THE NEW YORK
VOLUNTEER FIRE DEPARTMENT, ILLUSTRATIONS OF
OLD TIME FIRE SCENES, ETC.*

NEW YORK:

THOMAS BARRINGTON, PUBLISHER,

1887.

Press of
DAVID H. GILDERSLEEVE,
45 to 51 Rose St., N. Y.

VETERAN FIREMEN'S ASSOCIATION.

Officers, 1887.

GEORGE W. ANDERSON,	*President.*
JOHN MOLLER,	*1st Vice-President.*
ABRAM C. HULL,	*2d Vice-President.*
BERNARD M. SWEENY,	*Recording Secretary.*
A. T. ANDERSON,	*Financial Secretary.*
THOS. BARRINGTON,	*Corresponding Secretary.*
JAS. F. WENMAN,	*Treasurer.*
HENRY JONES,	*Sergt-at-Arms.*

Trustees.

FRED. A. RIDABOCK,	EUGENE WARD,	PETER P. PULLIS,
RICHARD H. NUGENT,	ABRAHAM SLAIGHT,	GEO. T. PATTERSON,
WM. McMAHON,	NELSON D. THAYER,	ROBT. McWHINNEY,
WM. B. DUNLEY,	T. DONOVAN,	THOS. BARRETT,
W. H. BOYD,	THOS. CLEARY,	THOS. LEAVY.

Committee on Entertainments.

GEORGE W. ANDERSON, *Chairman.*	THOMAS BARRINGTON, *Secretary.*
JAMES F. WENMAN,	GEO. T. PATTERSON,
NELSON D. THAYER,	WILLIAM McMAHON,
EUGENE WARD,	JOHN DAWSON.
THOMAS LEAVY.	

→ FIREMEN'S HALL ←

INTRODUCTION

HE Excursion that this little volume is designed to commemorate is the realization of the constant dream of the Volunteer Firemen. Trips by individual Companies to neighboring cities were of frequent occurrence during the existence of the old Department, but this limited sphere was not of sufficient scope to gratify the ambition and curiosity of the hardy veterans of many a well-fought conflagration.

They looked anxiously for the time when, as representatives of the New York Fire Department, they should be able to traverse the continent from New York to San Francisco by easy stages, to view the cities, mountains, valleys and plains of the United States, and especially to examine the facilities provided in different sections of the land for the irrepressible contest with that destructive element— fire, and also to exchange greetings with their brother firemen throughout the great West.

The rivalry existing between the Companies prevented the selection from the entire Department of a body to represent the New York organization, and no single Engine, Hose, or Hook and Ladder Company felt itself equal to so gigantic an undertaking as the transcontinental tour now to be taken by the Veteran Firemen's Association.

Nearly twenty-three years have elapsed since the disbandment of the old un-
paid force, after nearly two centuries of gratuitous service in the public interest, but
the *esprit de corps* did not disappear with the dissolution of the Association. The
old fire laddies have always cherished recollections of their arduous duties, which,
it must be acknowledged, were occasionally enlivened by set to's between rival
Companies, in their *futile* efforts to "pass" each other, and each Company had its
favorite meeting place, where the old-time fights with the flames and with each
other would be enthusiastically talked over. As is well known, this comradeship
resulted in the formation of the "Veteran Firemen's Association," with headquarters at No. 53 East Tenth Street, New York—the old Lorillard mansion. This
entire edifice is devoted to the club purposes of the institution. It is handsomely
furnished throughout, and every nook and corner contains a relic of the old Department, while the walls are hung with professional mementos and the portraits
of veteran firemen—some still living, but the greater number of whom has long
since passed to the tomb. Amid these reminiscent surroundings the members
gather in social intercourse, and forming in line before the door of these headquarters, the excursionists—one hundred in number—will start on their famous trip,
on Monday, September 5th, 1887.

The previous excursions of the Volunteers, above alluded to, are as follows:

Engine Company No. 6 to	.	.	.	.	Montreal.
" " " " "	.	.	.	.	Saratoga.
" " " 8 "	.	.	.	.	Washington.
" " " 11 "	.	.	.	.	Warren Monument.
" " " 33 "	.	.	.	.	Albany.
" " " 34 "	.	.	.	.	Washington.
" " " 38 "	.	.	.	.	New Haven.
" " " 40 "	.	.	.	.	Philadelphia.
" " " 44 "	.	.	.	.	"
" " " 51 "	.	.	.	.	Elmira.
Hose " " 5 "	.	.	.	.	New Haven.
" " " 16 "	.	.	.	.	Newburgh.
" " " 19 "	.	.	.	.	Buffalo.
" " " 22 "	.	.	.	.	Newark, N. J.
" " " 24 "	.	.	.	.	Newark.
" " " 25 "	.	.	.	.	Warren Monument.
Hook and Ladder Company No. 1 to .		.	.	New Haven.

The tourists look with special interest to their intended visit to the grave of DAVID C. BRODERICK, in Lone Mountain Cemetery, San Francisco, a New York fireman, who rose from the humblest position in life to that of Senator of the United States from California. Nearly 30 years have passed since he fell in the duel with Judge Terry, but his memory is still green in the hearts of those who knew him in his early manhood in New York, and many of the veterans who will look upon the monument that covers his remains will recall the time when they strove, side by side with him, to save life and property imperilled by the devouring element.

The following is the Itinerary:

MONDAY, SEPTEMBER 5th.—March down to the Battery, arriving there at 11 o'clock. Will then take special train at Weehawken for the West at 12 o'clock, arriving in Chicago at 4 P. M., September 6th, remaining during the entire day of the 7th, giving a Parade, and in the evening a Grand Concert and Reception, leaving for Omaha at midnight.

THURSDAY, SEPTEMBER 8th.—Arrive in Omaha at 4 P. M., and remain until midnight of the 9th, giving a Parade, and on the evening of the 9th a Grand Reception and Concert in the Exhibition Building.

SUNDAY, SEPTEMBER 11th.—Arrive in Salt Lake City at 5 P. M.

MONDAY, SEPTEMBER 12th.—Reception in Salt Lake City by the Municipal Government and Fire Department; viewing the interesting portions of Modern Zion; visit to the Great Salt Lake, and a Grand Concert in the great Tabernacle in the evening, leaving for California at midnight.

WEDNESDAY, SEPTEMBER 14th.—Arrive in Sacramento. Received by the local committees, Grand Parade, and a Reception and Concert in the evening.

THURSDAY, SEPTEMBER 15th.—Arrive in San Francisco. Received by the Exempt Fire Company and citizens generally, and Torchlight Parade in the evening.

FRIDAY, SEPTEMBER 16th.—Sight-seeing in San Francisco and Grand Concert and Reception in Grand Opera House in the evening.

SATURDAY AFTERNOON, SEPTEMBER 17th.—Grand Concert and Reception in Grand Opera House.

SUNDAY, SEPTEMBER 18th.—Leave San Francisco at 6 P. M. for Denver.

WEDNESDAY, SEPTEMBER 21st.—Arrive at Denver at 10 A. M. Parade, sight-seeing, and Grand Concert and Reception in the evening.

THURSDAY, SEPTEMBER 22d.—In Denver, sight-seeing and a good time. Leave for Kansas City at 9 P. M.

FRIDAY, SEPTEMBER 23d.—Arrive in Kansas City at 5 P. M.

SATURDAY, SEPTEMBER 24th.—In Kansas City. Parade and sight-seeing. Concert in the evening, and leave for St. Louis at midnight.

SUNDAY, SEPTEMBER 25th.—Arrive in St. Louis at 10 A. M.

MONDAY, SEPTEMBER 26th.—In St. Louis. Grand Parade, and in the evening Concert and Reception. Leave for Louisville at midnight.

TUESDAY, SEPTEMBER 27th.—Arrive at Louisville at 10 A. M. Grand Parade, and in the evening Grand Concert and Reception in Exhibition Building.

WEDNESDAY, SEPTEMBER 28th.—Leave Louisville at 9 A. M. Arrive in Cincinnati at 1 P. M. Parade to hotel, and in the evening Grand Concert and Reception at Exhibition Building.

THURSDAY, SEPTEMBER 29th.—Leave Cincinnati at 9 A. M. Arrive in Cleveland at 5 P. M. Parade to hotel, and in the evening Grand Concert in New Music Hall. Leave for Niagara Falls at 11 P. M.

SATURDAY, OCTOBER 1st.—Arrive at Niagara Falls at 6 A. M. "View the Falls." Leave at 8 A. M. for New York, arriving home at 8 P. M. All glad and happy and dusty and tired, and too full for utterance.

THE VETERAN FIREMEN'S ASSOCIATION

OF THE CITY OF NEW YORK.

T has always been a source of wonder and admiration with the public, how it is that the Old Firemen continue to maintain that *esprit de corps* so noted in the days of the late Volunteer Fire Department, so entirely their own and unknown in other bodies; it is a fact difficult to explain, for they certainly do retain a warm place in the hearts of the country which time appears rather to increase than diminish. It can, however, in a measure, be accounted for as follows:

Since the days of 1798 the Volunteer Fire Department has embraced among its members the very best classes of our citizens, and to-day they can be found throughout the walks of life of the entire world, still cherishing the same fraternal feeling for their old institution. Ministers to Foreign Countries, Judges, Mayors, prominent officials of all kinds, and millionaires without number, have once been Volunteer Firemen; their Initiation and Discharge Certificates occupy a prominent place in their homes, and cherished as proud mementos of the stirring and hazardous days of a Fireman, so fraught with danger as to be almost a fascination.

With this element permeating, as it were, *all* communities, it is hardly surprising
that the appearance of the Old Firemen should at once call forth spontaneous
applause; in fact, with *our* citizens, no *important* event in our Metropolis has ever
been considered complete without a representation from the Fire Department, which,
on such occasions, received the most *marked attention* from all classes of our citizens;
in fact, the Old Volunteer Firemen have always been *the* feature of all parades
in which they have participated, notably, the "Erie Canal Celebration," the "Reception of the Marquis de Lafayette," the "Croton Water Celebration," the "Reception of
the Prince of Wales," the "Celebration of the Laying of the Cable," the "Centennial Celebration of Evacuation day, 1883," and the "Inauguration of the Bartholdi Statue;"
the same pride and interest in everything pertaining to the old Department has been
perpetuated and kept alive by organizations of different associations.

Previous to our last Presidential election, a number of members of the old
Department met together to discuss the feasibility of forming an association for
the purpose of taking part in the next Presidential inauguration; the subject was
very favorably considered, and at a subsequent meeting, held in the early part of
September, 1884, an Association was formed for that purpose, under the name of
the "Veteran Firemen's Association," and the following Officers were selected for
the proposed trip, viz.:

GEORGE T. PATTERSON,	of Engine Co. 8,	Foreman.
WILLIAM B. DUNLEY,	" " " 6,	1st Assistant-Foreman.
PETER P. PULLIS,	" Hose Co. 40,	2d " "
LOUIS F. HALLEN,	" Engine Co. 34,	Treasurer.
JAMES H. BARTLEY,	" Hose Co. 1,	Secretary.

It took but a few days to fill the roll to the requisite number (200), and on the
morning of March 3d, 1885, they left the Grand Central Hotel, with 168 men on
the rope, clad in the old regulation uniform—Dark Blue Fire Coat and Pants, Red
Shirt, Black Neck-tie and regulation Fire Cap; they had with them a very handsome Double-deck Engine, belonging to Mr. John Moller (a member of the Association), who had purchased it in Philadelphia for this occasion.   Mr. George R.
Conner of Hose Co. 6 was appointed Marshal, and the following gentlemen Aids,
viz.: F. A. Ridabock of Hook and Ladder 12, John Moller of Engine 6, Louis
J. Parker of Engine 34, Eugene Ward of Engine 29, John McCauley of Engine
31, and Abraham Slaight of Hose 40, and the following Corps of Ex-Chief and

Assistant Engineers: Ex-Chief Engineer Harry Howard, Ex-Assistants Thos. Cleary, Bernard Kenny, and John B. Prote, Assistant-Engineer of Yonkers.

The march down Broadway was the commencement of an ovation which greeted them from their departure till their return.

At Washington, their reception was most enthusiastic; their splendid appearance calling forth encomiums from all, and they were assigned the second post of honor in the procession. On their return they were *captured* at Baltimore by the Baltimoreans, headed by their *whole-souled* Mayor, F. C. Latrobe (who was an old Volunteer Fireman), and tendered the Freedom of the City, and presented the Keys of the Public Institutions of Baltimore, and a memento of their visit, consisting of a highly burnished Copper Shield, 20x15 inches, in the shape of a Fire Cap Front, in the center of which is another Shield, silver-plated, with the following inscription:

KEYS OF THE CITY OF BALTIMORE,
Presented by the HON. F. C. LATROBE, Mayor,
To the VETERAN FIREMEN'S ASSOCIATION,
On their Visit to Baltimore and Washington,
March 3d, 4th and 5th, 1885.

Surrounding this are twelve keys, *fac-similes* of those of the public institutions of Baltimore, viz.: City Hall, Engine Houses, Station Houses, Parks, Theaters, Monuments, Churches, Penitentiary, Jail, Bay View, Night Key and the Key of the buildings of the Pennsylvania Railroad Company, to which is attached a Five-Cent Nickel Piece.   At each corner of the main Shield is a model of the Baltimore Monument, and at the top is a pair of Clasped Hands.   A silver-plated American Eagle, perched on a globe, with red, white and blue streamers floating from its beak, surmounts the brass standard to which the Shield is attached.

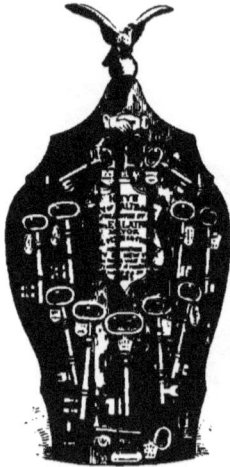

The Mayor, in making the presentation, alluded in flattering terms to the Volunteer Firemen of New York, who had ever had a warm place in the heart of the Baltimoreans.

Ex-Chief Engineer Harry Howard responded in behalf of the Association in his usual happy and felicitous manner, which drew plaudits from the surrounding throng.

At Philadelphia, they received another flattering and enthusiastic reception.   They arrived in that city at 9 o'clock on the evening of March 6th, and were received by the Volunteer Firemen's Association of that City and escorted through the principal streets to the Bound Brook Hotel, where a magnificent banquet was given, the Hon. William Mann, of Philadelphia, delivering the Address of Welcome, which was responded to, on behalf of the Association, by Ex-Chief Harry Howard, Geo. T. Patterson, George W. Anderson, George R. Conner and others, after which they marched to the Bingham House and put up for the night.   The next morning a breakfast was served at Donaldson's, after which the Volunteer Firemen's Association escorted them to the different places of interest about the city, including Wannemaker's, U. S. Mint, New City Hall, winding up by marching with them to the Pennsylvania Railroad Dépot.   On the route they received the same flattering attention, and their arrival home was marked by a welcome such as Firemen only know how to give.   Soon after their arrival, Mr. Dorsey, the proprietor of Barnum's City Hotel, at Baltimore, forwarded a beautiful Standard of Blue Silk, with the Coat of arms of the City of Baltimore embroidered thereon, as a slight token of his esteem and as a memento of their visit to the Monumental City. The happy associations of old friends thus revived were more firmly cemented by this short trip, and it was resolved to make the organization a permanent one. A call was accordingly made for a meeting to be held on March 15th, 1885, which was largely attended, and it was unanimously resolved to organize permanently under the name of the "Veteran Firemen's Association," and the following named gentlemen were unanimously elected the Officers :

George W. Anderson,	of Hose 22,	President.
John Moller,	of Engine 6,	Vice-President.
James F. Wenman,	Ex-Assistant-Engineer,	Treasurer.
Bernard M. Sweeny,	of Engine 39,	Recording Secretary.
James H. Bartley,	of Hose 1,	Financial Secretary.
Henry Jones,	of Engine 40,	Sergeant-at-Arms.

Board of Trustees.—Fred. A. Ridabock, Hook and Ladder 12 ; John Tuomey, Engine 7 ; Thomas Barrett, Engine 12 ; Abram C. Hull, Hook and Ladder 13 ; Edward Bonnell, Hose 16 ; Eugene Ward, Engine 29 ; Henry Gunther, Hose 4 ; Abraham Slaight, Hose 40 ; William Orford, Hose 58 ; Daniel Quinn, Engine 3 ; Thomas Cleary, Engine 20 ; Daniel Garvey, Hose 6 ; Richard Evans, Engine 6 ; G. T. Patterson, Engine 8 ; Patrick Daily, Engine 17, with a rank and file of 250 members.

The object of the formation of the organization being to renew the social intercourse that existed in the old Volunteer Department, a Committee was appointed to select suitable Headquarters. They succeeded in securing the old family mansion of the Lorillards', located at 53 East Tenth Street, near Broadway. The building is a four story Brown Stone Front, 28 feet wide by 80 feet deep. The Committee were instructed to fit it up as a Club House, regardless of expense, and it is furnished from top to bottom in the most luxurious style, with library, reading-rooms, billiard-rooms, restaurant, and every convenience of a first-class Club. The house contains many cherished relics of the old Department.

The parlors contain several very costly Oil Paintings and Steel Engraved Portraits of old Firemen, among which may be mentioned those of Ex-Assistant Engineer James F. Wenman and Edward W. Jacobs, executed in oil by that eminent Artist, Joseph H. Johnson, and presented to the Association by their many friends and admirers. Also very large-sized Crayons of their President, Mr. George

CLUB HOUSE.

W. Anderson, Vice-President John Moller, Frederick A. Ridabock, Eugene Ward, and Portraits in Oil of Ex-Chief Engineers James Gulick and Harry Howard, Ex-Engineer John B. Miller, Matthew T. Brennan, Ex-Foreman of Engine 21, Henry S. Mansfield, Ex-Foreman of Hose 9, David C. Broderick, Ex-Foreman of Engine 34,

Wm. A. Woodhull, Ex-Foreman of Hose 36, Ex-Alderman Wesley Smith, of Hydrant Co. No. 4, and many others.

Under the indefatigable exertions of its popular President, Mr. George W. Anderson, the Association now numbers over 500 members.

Among the many reminiscences of the old Department, none have left a more pleasant and lasting impression than the Annual Balls given by the Firemen's Ball Committee, in aid of the Widow and Orphans Benevolent Fund (a brief history of which is given elsewhere), and as most of the members of that Committee are now members of this Association, it was decided to revive the custom, and the Metropolitan Opera House was engaged for the first Ball, which took place on Tuesday Evening, Jan. 12th, 1886, and was a most brilliant success in every particular, and placed it at once in the front ranks of the Terpsichorean festivities of the City. Previous to the opening of the Ball, two beautiful gold badges, set in diamonds, were presented to the President, George W. Anderson, and Vice-President John Moller. The second Annual Ball was given at the same place on Tuesday Evening, Jan. 18th, 1887, and (if such a thing were possible) was even more brilliant than its predecessor. A number of private boxes, beautifully decorated, were set apart for representatives from the veteran "Old Guard" of this City, the Veteran Firemen's Associations from Baltimore, Washington, Philadelphia, New Haven, Jamaica, Hoboken and Brooklyn, Phœnix Hose Co. of Poughkeepsie and Continental Hose of Elizabeth.

Before commencing the festivities of the evening, the members of the Volunteer Firemen's Association of Brooklyn, through their respected President, Judge Courtney, presented the Association with a slight memorial of friendship and esteem, in the shape of a large Fire Cap Front of highly polished copper, with silver mountings, beautifully encased in a gilt frame, with the following inscription thereon :

Presented to THE VETERAN FIREMEN'S ASSOCIATION
of the City of New York,
by the
BROOKLYN VOLUNTEER FIREMEN'S ASSOCIATION
of the City of Brooklyn, W. D.,
January 18, 1887.

" Ein Dracht Macht Macht."
B. V. F. A.

The speech of the Judge was in his usual able and happy strain.   President
Anderson received this token of brotherhood as another binding link of good
fellowship. (This beautiful memento now adorns the walls of the parlor at headquarters.)

There was always one characteristic of the old Firemen ; that was, to be kept
thoroughly posted as to what was occurring in different parts of the country re-
lating to fire matters.   The same holds good now, and the thorough and successful
organization of the Veterans was followed by invitations from various Fire Depart-
ments to visit their cities and take part in the Annual Parades.   Of course, many
had to be refused, but they have taken part in enough to keep them pretty well
employed, the most notable of which were the following :

The parade of the Jamaica Fire Department, when they, with 100 men, were
enthusiastically received by the Authorities and Fire Department and entertained
royally, and left carrying with them the good wishes of all.

Their next visit was to Bayonne, N. J., Oct. 7th, 1885, on invitation of the
Bayonne Fire Department, where they were the recipients of hospitalities from the
citizens generally, and while they were the guests of the Fire Department, the
ladies of the city considered them their special guests.   The Company numbered
175 men ; they were met at Bergen Point, on arrival of the boat, by committees
from the City Authorities, Fire Department, Bayonne Athletic Club, and Argonaut
Boat Club, and escorted to a bounteous repast, after partaking of which the line
of march was formed, the Veterans being courteously given the right of the line.
(The wives and families of the members who had accompanied them on the boat

were taken in charge by the ladies of Bayonne and made to feel a New Jersey greeting.) The city presented a holiday appearance, and banners—"Welcome to Veterans of New York"—met you at every turn; in fact, the applause and reception all along the line of march was such as would lead one to suppose the parade to be entirely in honor of the Veterans, which was still further strengthened by a shower of presentations, for before the line of march was taken up the Veterans were drawn up in front of a Grand Stand, when Mayor Henry Meigs presented the Association with a Red Silk Banneret from the Athletic Club of Bayonne, a White Silk Banneret from the Argonaut Boat Club, and a most superb Silk American Flag from the Bayonne Fire Department, and a small cannon presented by Miss May A. Wildey; these gifts were feelingly received by President Anderson, when *another* surprise took the genial President unawares and he called Ex-Engineer Jas. F. Wenman to the front to receive from Mrs. Henry Meigs, on behalf of the ladies of Bayonne, a beautiful Banner of Blue Silk, handsomely Embroidered. It is needless to say the Veterans returned to the city heavy laden with the kindness of the citizens of Bayonne, and with hearts full of most pleasant recollections.

Phœnix Hose Co., of Poughkeepsie, making a trip to Boston, decided to make a short stop in this City on their way home, which, coming to the ears of the Veterans, they decided to try and capture them for a few hours. Their manner of doing so is best shown in the following clipping from one of the daily papers :

RECEPTION TO PHŒNIX HOSE.

A Reception was tendered the Phœnix Hose No. 1 (the Swell Company) of Poughkeepsie, at the Parlors in Tenth Street, on their return from Boston. They were met at Fall River by over eighty members of the Veteran Association. On landing in New York the visitors were escorted to the Astor House, where a breakfast was given by Mr. Allen, the proprietor, who was formerly a resident of Poughkeepsie. The party then, accompanied by the band and the handsome $3,500 parade carriage of the Phœnix, proceeded up Broadway, attracting great attention and frequent applause. The visitors were made welcome at the Club Rooms and enjoyed themselves socially until 2 o'clock, when lunch was served.

The basement had been turned into a banquet-room, and over 200 jolly fire laddies sat down to do justice to the sumptuous repast under which the tables groaned, and the laddies smiled under the influence of champagne. The toast was proposed by President Anderson, "The Volunteer Fire Department of Poughkeepsie—May its members continue to enjoy the respect and esteem of the citizens in their laudable efforts in saving life and protecting property from the fiery elements." Mr. Brown, of the Poughkeepsie *Enterprise*, responded.

The President then proposed the toast: "Phœnix Hose No. 1, who derived their name from the bird that arises from its own ashes with renewed life. So may their organization rise triumphant over every difficulty with renewed life for further exertions in the sacred cause to which they are devoted." Mayor White (who is an old fireman and is president of the Poughkeepsie College) responded in a witty and happy strain.

The President of the Veterans then presented Chief Kaess with a fire hat on behalf of the organization. The Chief, who is a jolly big fellow, declared he would wear it on every occasion and would never disgrace it.

"Foreman Van Kleeck's head has grown since this hat was made for him," said the Chairman, holding up a silver toy fire hat, "but in the hope that it will expand when directly subjected to the influence of his large brain, I present it to him on behalf of the Veteran Firemen's Association of the City of New York."

Mr. Van Kleeck said he was not a speaker, but would call for three cheers for the Veteran Firemen's Association of New York. The banquet-hall echoed with the thundering response. The Poughkeepsie boys took the Hudson River boat at 4 o'clock for Kingston, where they were warmly received and then proceeded home.

This pleasant entertainment was soon followed by a special invitation from "Phœnix Hose Co. No. 1," to take part in the Annual Parade of the Poughkeepsie Fire Department and be their "Guests." As a refusal would not be considered, the Veterans mustered 200 men and chartered the Steamboat "Crystal Stream," arriving at Poughkeepsie in the early evening, and such a reception as they received has never been seen on this continent. An old-fashion Torchlight Parade had been arranged to welcome the Vets; on landing at the wharf they were met by Phœnix Hose Co. No. 1 and the entire Fire Department, headed by that prince of whole-souled firemen, Chief-Engineer Kaess, and started on the march.

The Veterans had seen and taken part in nearly all of the Torchlight Parades in this country and many had seen them in all parts of Europe, but "Poughkeepsie" *eclipsed them all.* From the landing at the foot of the hill to the end of the march, a distance of about four miles, the streets were literally on fire. The Vets had often been singed in fighting fire, but here they were called upon to get singed in marching through "Fires of Welcome." No pen can describe that sight, but one can imagine what it might be, with Tar Barrels, stationed 10 feet apart on both sides of the street, ablaze, and from every house on the route fireworks, Red and Blue Lights burning from every window, Companies of Infantry firing their rifles from their armories, and every foot of ground on sidewalks crowded with citizens, aglow with excitement and enthusiasm, and you can form a slight idea of the "Welcome to the Veterans" displayed on all sides. After the Parade they were entertained at a Banquet given in the Town Hall, presided over by the Mayor of Poughkeepsie, who, on behalf of the City Authorities, tendered them the freedom of the City. Quarters were provided at the Nelson House and Morgan Hotel, and the house of Phœnix Hose Co. placed at their disposal.

The following day the Vets were assigned the right of the line in the Annual Parade of the Poughkeepsie Department, when they received another perfect ovation and were the center of attraction. Their appearance elicited universal admiration. Another banquet and a parting Good-Bye at the house of their friends (Phœnix Hose), they took their steamer, and with Band playing "Auld Lang Syne" and amidst waving of handkerchiefs and booming of cannon they bade adieu to their hosts, thus cementing another link of brotherhood. "Home again"—but they were not to be allowed to seek their homes quietly, for the Veteran Firemen's "Sons" thought they would give the old gentlemen a reception, and met them at the wharf and escorted them to headquarters; the citizens along the route thought they would have something to say about it and welcomed them with a grand display of Fireworks up to the doors of headquarters. In passing the armory of the Old Guard a hearty Welcome Home resounded therefrom. This closed one of the most enjoyable of trips, leaving nothing but sweet recollections.

At the recent inaugural ceremonies of the Bartholdi Statue the Association took a prominent part. This event showed how dear to the hearts of the people the memory of the old Volunteer Firemen clung. No greater assemblage of people ever gathered in our City than on that day, to witness the Military, Civic, and Volunteer Firemen parade. The Military and Civic portion received plaudits, but nothing like enthusiasm was exhibited until the column of the Volunteer Firemen came in sight, when one continuous outbreak of enthusiasm followed them through the entire line of march. The Veterans received marked attention from the assembled multitude, and in passing the Grand Reviewing Stand received a noticeable acknowledgment from President Cleveland remarking to one of his staff that he remembered that Company as being present at his inaugural.

The Association paraded 217 men on the rope in full uniform, preceded by Diller's band of 60 pieces. The Corps of Engineers consisted of Ex-Chief Harry Howard, with the Chief-Engineers of Poughkeepsie, Plainfield and Yonkers, Ex-Assistant Engineers James F. Wenman, Elisha Kingsland, Edward W. Jacobs, Thomas Cleary and John H. Foreman. Their beautiful engine (which had been purchased by the Association from Mr. John Moller and redecorated and painted at great expense) fairly outshone itself, and on the top gallery was mounted a fine Bronze Statue of Liberty Enlightening the World.

The Association had as guests on that occasion, to whom they acted as an Escort, the following Companies:

The Veteran Volunteer Firemen's Association of Philadelphia, Veteran Volunteer Firemen's Association of Baltimore, the Continental Hose Co. of Elizabeth, N. J., the Exempt Firemen's Association of Brooklyn, E. D., the Volunteer Firemen's Association of Brooklyn, and delegates from Phœnix Hose Co. No. 1 of Poughkeepsie, whom they entertained at a banquet in the evening at Irving Hall, at which 600 persons sat down.

The occasion was a most enjoyable one, and it was with reluctance that the time was announced for a separation, previous to which, however, the Baltimore and Elizabeth visitors presented the Veterans with their Banners and Flags as mementos of the occasion.

It was at this gathering, in talking over the olden times and various excursions taken by different companies, and of the wishes so often expressed to make a trip to the Golden Gate, that the proposed trip of the Veterans to California took birth, and at the next meeting a Committee, consisting of Thomas Barrington, James F. Wenman and Nelson D. Thayer were appointed to report upon the feasibility of making such a tour. Taking the matter at once in hand, at the succeeding meeting they unanimously recommended such a trip, which report was warmly approved by the Association and a resolution adopted, referring it to the following committee to make all arrangements for what bids fair to be the most gigantic and successful trip ever made across our continent. The Committee consists of Messrs. George W. Anderson, Thomas Barrington, James F. Wenman, Nelson D. Thayer, George T. Patterson, William McMahon, Eugene Ward, John Dawson and Thomas Leavy.

But while indulging in pleasure and festivities they have not lost sight of their other less fortunate brother firemen, but quietly performed one of the most benevolent acts ever undertaken in the Department. The want of a Home for the poor and distressed firemen has long been felt, and while our city abounds in Homes for the poor and distressed, the Firemen appear to have been forgotten. The subject was brought to the attention of the Association by President Anderson, and a Charter was at once obtained for the establishing of such a Home, to be known as the "Veteran Firemen's Home Association."

On the afternoon of Thursday, May 26th, 1887, the Veteran Volunteer Fire-men's Association of the City of Brooklyn, of which Mr. James A. Walsh is President, paraded through New York City with their beautiful double-deck hand Engine which they had just received from the decorators, and passed through East Tenth Street, their intention being to give the Veterans a marching salute, but the Veterans determined to outflank them, if possible, so they quietly blocked the street and captured the entire party, band and drum corps included, and marched them into the Club House, and there set them down to a table loaded with good things calculated to appease hunger and quench thirst, after which the Veterans, some seventy in number, clad in full fire rig, escorted them to the Battery and saw them safely aboard the South Ferry boat and sent them on their way rejoicing ; but the Brooklyn Vets were not to be outdone so easily, so on Wednesday Evening, August 3d, while the regular Meeting of the Veterans was in session, they were suddenly interrupted in their proceedings by a large delegation, headed by Mr. Munson S. Brown (who, by the way, is also a member of our own Association), bearing with them a beautifully engrossed set of resolutions, surrounded by an elegant gold frame, thanking the Veterans for courtesies extended, and promising to behave themselves the next time they visited New York, and not try to *pass* them in their own street.

From Sheldon's "Story of Volunteer Fire Department."

Copyright, 1889, by Harper & Brothers.

THE VETERANS PICTURE

D. H. ANDERSON, Photographer.   MARCH 7TH, 1885.

THE VETERANS PICTURE

FTER the return of the Veterans from their trip to Washington, where they assisted at the inauguration of the President of the United States, on March 4th, 1885, they resolved to commemorate the incident of their presence at the Capital of the country on that memorable occasion, by a picture of the group. In order to secure strict accuracy, every member of the party called at the studio of the artist, Mr. D. H. Anderson, at No. 785 Broadway, himself an old Volunteer Fireman, and were photographed singly. To infuse prominent features of New York City street life into the scene, newsboys and a bootblack were taken to the gallery and their likenesses also secured in professional attire and position. A photograph of the Engine was then taken and the presentments of the Veterans were then arranged in their proper places, as they appeared in the triumphal march up Broadway on their return from Washington on the afternoon of March 7th. The site selected for the illustration of the work was the famous thoroughfare at the north-west corner of the City Hall Park. In the middle ground, partly hidden by venerable trees, are seen the Old City Hall, the County Court House, and other municipal buildings. In the background, on Park Row and Beekman Street, are the *Tribune* and Potter buildings, and Temple Court, all triumphs of architectural skill, while a portion of the Post Office looms up at the south, and Chambers Street, with the Stewart Building and other commercial edifices, appears on the north. The features of the Veterans and bystanders are brought out with speaking exactitude, and the entire picture, which is 12 feet long by 8 feet wide, and handsomely framed, vividly recalls the noted trip of which it is a souvenir. Many copies have been taken for the Veterans and their friends, and adorn the walls of their homes or places of business.

⚬ PHŒNIX ⚬ HOSE ⚬ CO. ⚬ NO. ⚬ 1. ⚬

A Complete Description of Phœnix Hose Co. Carriage.   Nearly all Gold, Silver, Steel and Glass.
Built by W. W. Wunder, of Reading, Pa.   Fancy Work by Devoosney Bros., New York.
Received by Phœnix Hose Co. on September 4th, 1884.

THE Carriage stands 11 feet 5 inches high from the floor to top of figure
over the reel, and, with the exceptions of the wheels and tongue and
lockers, which are of wood, is entirely constructed of gold, silver, steel
and glass.   The wheels stand 5 feet 6 inches and 5 feet 8 inches high.
They are of the Archibald pattern, with gold hubs.   The tongue is of
hickory, elegantly carved; the handles, etc., being of silver.   The wheels
and tongue are painted carmine and gold, and are the only parts of the Carriage
that are painted.   The axles, reach, arches, springs, etc., are of the best polished

steel, silver-plated, not electro-plated, but hand-plated. The reel heads are of glass, cut and designed in the most costly manner. In each reel-head are eight panels cut in the glass, and in each panel is cut a glass ornament as follows : In the top panel the Coat of arms of the State of New York ; in the bottom panel, the Coat of arms of the City of Poughkeepsie ; in the left hand panel is a *fac-simile* of the old Carriage of *"Phœnix"*; in the right are the fire emblems— Hat, Trumpet, Pipe, Torch and Lamp, and in the four intervening panels are cut emblems representing the four seasons of the year—Spring, Summer, Autumn, and Winter. In the center of each reel-head is placed a gold hydrant, full size, and by unscrewing the caps, the cranks can be put on and hose reeled on, if neces- sary. On ground work, underneath the hydrant, is the word " Phœnix " in raised gold letters. The lockers are of rose-wood framed with gold, and in each end is a cut-glass ornament. The figures on the front represents two Rescues, viz. : Fireman rescuing a Child from a burning building, and Dog rescuing a Child from the water. The rear ones represent the Goddess of Liberty, and Female riding an Eagle through the ˙clouds. The lifters are elegant, gold equestrian statues, and represent ancient chargers, Knight and Horse. On the front are the words "Organized, 1844," and in the rear, " Poughkeepsie," in raised gold letters. The side arches are of a new and beautiful design, and something never before seen on a hose carriage. They are heavily silver-plated, and on the top center of each stands a gold-plated statue, representing an Amazon holding in one hand a small lamp of unique design and in the other holding a spear and shield. On the center of a bar which goes over the reel stands a silver figure 37 inches high, representing Flying Mercury. The original bronze figure was brought from Paris by R. R. Dennis, Esq., one of the Committee.

The Jacket or Apron is of silver, secured by two gold bands, the borders of which are splendidly engraved. On the front is a Monogram of the Company, all in raised letters, and on the rear is a large Phœnix bird in raised gold.

The front and rear signal frames, bell galleries, scrolls, etc., are of silver. The front has three signal lamps, and the rear two. The lamps are of silver, and of the finest pattern that can be produced. The large one in front is mounted with an American Eagle in gold, and the others with gold Phœnix birds. On the center of the back arch is a silver figure of old " Neptune." Underneath the signals hang two handsome silver hand-lamps. In the front bell gallery are two silver bells of the Lily pattern, and between the bells and directly underneath the center signal hangs a silver sea shell, in the center of which is the figure 1, and surrounded by the motto of the Company—" Fearless and Faithful," and immediately underneath hangs a silver plate with this inscription :

O. H. Booth, Foreman, 1844.

Wm. Kaess, Chief-Engineer, 1884.

There are also two silver play-pipes across the front scroll end and two silver rollers across the rear end, each one fastened by a gold rosette.   The rope reel is of silver.   On each side is a gold wreath, and when the rope is reeled up and the cranks are taken off, there will be screwed on in their places two gold tiger heads.   The other ornaments, which are numerous, are all of gold.

From the above description it will be seen that the whole make up of the Carriage is of the best and most costly character.   The total cost of the Carriage is $3,000, and is the property of Phœnix Hose Co., No. 1.

From Sheldon's " Story of Volunteer Fire Department "   Copyright, 1882, by Harper & Brothers.

A NEW YORK FIRE SCENE—1733.

THE ASSOCIATION OF EXEMPT FIREMEN
. OF . THE . CITY . OF . NEW . YORK .

GEORGE W. WHEELER.

ON the evening of October 13th, 1842, the Association of Exempt Firemen was organized for the purpose of protecting the Benevolent Fund of the Volunteer Fire Department. There having been, even at that early date, some talk of instituting a paid Fire Department, the Volunteer Firemen were naturally anxious about the future of the Fund which their charitable energies had provided for the widows and orphans. The meeting was held at Monroe Hall, at the corner of Centre and Pearl Streets, and Mr. Edward Dayton was called to the chair and Mr. Neil Gray appointed Secretary.

On motion, Ex-Chief-Engineer Uzziah Wenman was made President, Ex-Chief-Engineer James Gulick, First Vice-President, Ex-Chief-Engineer John Riker, Jr., Second Vice-President, and Mr. Neil Gray Secretary and Treasurer.

On the 13th day of October, 1843, the organization changed its name to "The Association of Exempt Firemen of the City of New York," whose object was "to afford such aid to the Fire Department of the City of New York as lies in our power, and also to cherish and perpetuate the kind feeling and social intercourse which have heretofore existed among us as Firemen." The phrase " Exempt Firemen," it was explained, meant that the Firemen had served a sufficient time to exempt them "from other public duties and to entitle them, should occasion require, to assistance from the funds of the Fire Department." Any Exempt Fireman might become a member of the Association by paying an initiation fee of fifty cents and by subscribing to the articles. The time for the annual meeting was the third Tuesday in January; but on the 13th of May, 1844, it was resolved to meet every three months, viz.: on the third Tuesday in January, April, July and October. In 1849, the initiation fee was increased to one dollar; it is now ten dollars. In 1851, Mr. George W. Wheeler, the Secretary, reported that the total number of members was two hundred and ninety. The number now on the roll is nearly seven hundred.

After the disbandment of the Volunteer Fire Department, the Legislature enacted that the President and two Vice-Presidents of the Association of Exempt Firemen, together with the Trustees of the Fire Department Fund, should constitute a body corporate and politic by the name and style of "The Trustees of the Exempt Firemen's Benevolent Fund of the City of New York," and that this body should have charge of that Fund and also of the Firemen's Monument and ground at Greenwood Cemetery. It was further enacted that the Association of Exempt Firemen "shall have a right to inquire into and control the application of said Fund and revenue, to displace any Officer or Trustee guilty of misconduct, and to elect others in their stead." To these duties the Association has ever since addressed itself.

OFFICERS FOR 1887.

PRESIDENT.

ZOPHAR MILLS. *

EDMUND STEPHENSON, *First Vice-President.* PETER MASTERSON, *Second Vice-President.*
GEO. W. WHEELER, *Recording Secretary.* FRANCIS HAGADORN, *Financial Secretary.*

TREASURER.

ANTHONY C. D'OZEVILLE.

EXECUTIVE COMMITTEE.

JOSEPH D. COSTA,   ROBERT C. ARMSTRONG,
ELISHA KINGSLAND,   HUGH CURRY,
DANIEL MOONEY,   CHRIS. JOHNSON,
ROBERT I. LOMAS,   WILLIAM B. DUNLEY,

JOSEPH D. COSTA, *Sergeant-at-Arms.*

TRUSTEES OF THE EXEMPT FIREMEN'S BENEVOLENT FUND.

JOHN J. GORMAN, *President.*   JOHN J. TINDALE, *Secretary.*
ROBERT C. ARMSTRONG, *Treasurer.*   FREDERICK A. RIDABOCK,
WILLIAM SWINERTON,   EUGENE WARD,
ANTHONY YEOMAN,   EDWARD W. JACOBS,
RICHARD EVANS,   LOUIS J. BELLONI, JR.,
JAMES Y. WATKINS,   THOMAS F. RILEY,
JAMES B. MINGAY,   GEORGE KILLING.
      * Died.

THE • FIREMEN'S • BALL • COMMITTEE.

HE Volunteer Fire Department of the City of New York was disbanded in 1865. During the many years of its existence as an organization, its wonderful efficiency was generally recognized and acknowledged, and it was at once the pride and boast of the Citizens of the Metropolis. Historians have recorded the self-sacrificing endeavors, the heroic deeds, the hair-breadth escapes, and in many cases the deeds of valor performed by the members, while Poets have sung of their glorious achievements, and, when the sad occasion required, have woven Poetic wreaths to the memory of the gallant and illustrious dead.

At an early date in the history of the Department (1792) it was found necessary that some provision should be made to care for the sick and disabled firemen, as well as to provide for the comfort of the widow and orphan of deceased members, to this end a Fund was established, known as the "Fire Department Fund," which was incorporated March 20th, 1798, and placed under the control of Trustees to carry out the object for which it was created. For a number of years the demands upon the Fund were few and far between, but, as the years rolled on, and the calls became more frequent, it became apparent that some other means must be adopted that would materially augment the income of the Fund and enable the Trustees to meet the increased demand upon their finances. The outcome of this was the organization of the "Firemen's Ball Committee."

In the year 1829, a number of gentlemen, prominent as citizens and connected with the Fire Department, deeply impressed with the necessity of increasing the revenue of the Fund, after many meetings and much deliberation, organized themselves into an Association, for the purpose of giving an Annual Ball, the proceeds of which should be turned over to the Fund; their aims and objects are best set forth by the publication of the following Preamble which they adopted:

"WHEREAS, The Fire Department Fund was instituted for the purpose of affording relief to such members of the Fire Department as may stand in need of assistance, and to alleviate the wants and distresses of the widows and orphans of deceased Firemen; and

"WHEREAS, The ordinary receipts of the Fund have been found to be insufficient to meet the increasing demands upon it, a number of individuals, impelled by feelings of philanthropy and benevolence, having formed themselves into a Committee for the purpose of giving an Annual Ball, and with the view of perpetuating it, and for the better government of the Committee, the present members have deemed it advisable to form the following code of By-Laws:"

At this period, many of the most prominent citizens of New York who were connected with the Department, were most active in the discharge of their duty, and foremost in every work of benevolence. The originators of this Committee were of this class of citizens. They took hold of the matter with the determination that it should be a success, and a success it was from the inception. Their first Ball was given at the Bowery Theater, in January, 1830, and was to a great extent experimental. The price of tickets was fixed at two dollars, and the net proceeds were $199.20. Encouraged by their first experiment, the Committee redoubled their efforts (increasing the price of tickets to five dollars) and were gratified to find their labors appreciated. The Balls were patronized and attended by the wealth, beauty and fashion of city and suburbs. No public balls given at this date can in any way be brought in favorable comparison with them. The demand for tickets increased with each year, and as the number was always limited, it was frequently the case that none were to be obtained on the day of the Ball, and as high a premium as twenty-five dollars has been offered for them.

The continued and unvarying success of the Balls was due, to a great extent, to the care exercised by the Committee in the prevention of the admission of improper characters to the building upon the occasion of a Ball. Each member was compelled to keep a list of the names of parties to whom tickets were sold, and in this manner became, to some extent, personally responsible for the standing and character of his own friends, as well as those who accompanied them. A strict surveillance was observed by the Police Committee, and in the event of the introduction of a person of questionable repute her escort was at once directed to remove her from the building. It is needless to add, that this order was immediately complied with in all such cases; though, fortunately, there were but few. The further penalty was attached to the offending party of prohibiting him from ever thereafter participating in the pleasures of a Firemen's Ball.

As previously stated, the First Annual Ball was given at the Bowery Theater, and the price of tickets were two dollars, admitting a gentlemen and ladies. This Ball was experimental, and the Committee gained wisdom by experience. They increased the price of tickets to five dollars, and successively engaged the Park Theater (then on Park Row), the National Theater, Astor Place Opera House, Niblo's, and the Academy of Music. The success of the Balls continued unabated until some years after the disbandment of the Department. For this success the members of the Committee labored with unflagging zeal. To them it was indeed a labor of love; the object was one dear to their hearts, and they threw their souls into their work in the fond endeavor to make each recurring Ball a greater success than its predecessor. Their wishes could not always be gratified, as may be seen from the financial statement below. The first three years of the late War militated against them, but when the last vestige of the unpleasantness had passed away, they made a renewed and determined effort, and, in 1868, succeeded in increasing the net proceeds to the magnificent sum of $6,244.08. The brilliant success of the 39th Annual Ball will live long in the memory of those who were members of the Committee at that time. It was the first year of the Presidency of Mr. James F. Wenman, and the Treasurership of Mr. Alonzo Slote, and the individual celebration of the event by the latter gentleman will ever be a pleasing reminiscence to those who were the partakers of his bounteous hospitality.

The last Ball of the very successful series was given in 1873, and was in

every way, except possibly in point of numbers present, worthy of its predecessors, and was a brilliant termination to the labors of the Committee, who had by this time decided that it was advisable, for various reasons, to discontinue the Balls and retire upon their laurels. It might be well to note here that from the commencement to the close, the members invariably paid for their own tickets of admission. The only invitations extended by the Committee were to Gen. Winfield Scott, and David T. Valentine, for many years Clerk of the Common Council, except in the cases of Mr. Chas. Dickens, who was invited to attend the 13th, and Prince Arthur, of England, who was invited to attend the 41st Annual Ball.

The following exhibit will show the net proceeds of each Ball, from 1830 to 1873 :

YEAR.	AMOUNT.	YEAR.	AMOUNT.	YEAR.	AMOUNT.
1830	$ 199 20	1844	$1,376 37	1859	$4,924 37
1831	824 15	1845	1,719 65	1860	2,411 77
1832	631 35	1846	2,013 14	1861	2,792 30
1833	1,001 97	1847	1,880 40	1862	3,274 30
1834	1,100 33	1848	2,156 17	1863	5,275 13
1835	1,286 24	1849	2,338 04	1864	5,824 67
1836	1,135 19	1850	2,993 93	1865	5,911 13
1837 Ryker.	1,311 19	1851	3,349 38	1866	5,636 84
1837 Gul'ck.	1,208 91	1852	3,031 09	1867	5,372 83
1838	1,346 62	1853	3,385 82	1868	6,244 08
1839	1,911 98	1854	3,839 05	1869	5,466 61
1840	1,363 82	1855	3,956 34	1870	3,298 42
1841	1,184 63	1856	4,955 69	1871	3,301 88
1842	1,274 55	1857	5,399 31	1872	1,000 00
1843	1,275 43	1858	4,744 10	1873	1,000 00

Making a grand total of $125,928.37 contributed to the Benevolent Fund of the Fire Department, through the medium of this Committee.

In the Fall of 1878, the Southern portion of our country was ravaged by that fearful scourge —Yellow Fever.   Commerce was paralyzed, business was entirely suspended, and desolation stalked throughout the land.   The demands for financial aid were constant and pressing.   The·North gave liberally of its treasure; but the cry was still for more!   Nor was the cry unheeded : Charity sounded the alarm, and the Ball Committee promptly responded to the call, with their old time fervor.   Within a few days they completed preparations for a monster Concert for the Benefit of the Sufferers.   Musical talent of the highest order was placed at their disposal ; the services of eminent Artists were secured, and Madison Square Garden was rented for the occasion.   Again did success crown their efforts.   The large Garden was filled to overflowing, fully eight thousand persons being present, and the handsome sum of $5,462 realized, which was distributed among the several cities where it was considered aid was most needed.   The acknowledgment from the officials of these cities was most gratifying to the Committee, and fully repaid them for their efforts and labor.   Subsequently, a Resolution was adopted thanking the Artists and others for their services in promoting the success of the Concert—though aware that each and every one will find greater reward in the knowledge that their charitable act will carry comfort to many a sorrowing home, and always remembering that—

> " No radiant pearl that crested fortune wears,
> Nor twinkling gem that hangs from beauty's ears;
> Not all the stars that night's blue arch adorn,
> Nor e'en the rising sun that gilds the vernal morn,
> Shines with such luster as does the tear that flows
> Down virtue's manly check for others woes."

This was the last public entertainment given under the auspices of the Committee.   The organization is, however, still continued, and its festivities are confined to an Excursion in the Summer, and a grand Dinner on the 16th of December, the Anniversary of the great fire of 1835, holding themselves, however, in readiness, should circumstances warrant or occasion require their services, to renew the successes of their earlier days.   The Committee elects no new members ; it proposes to have its annual festivities so long as there are two members left.

The records of the Committee are rich in the names of the many prominent and well known citizens who have been active in its Councils during the 58 years of its existence.   As Presidents, they have had the valuable services of Uzziah

Wenman, Chief-Engineer of the Department, and father of the present President, of James Gulick, also Chief-Engineer, and a general favorite, of Cornelius V. Anderson, Chief-Engineer and President of the Lorillard Insurance Company, of Henry A. Burr, a distinguished New York Merchant, of C. Godfrey Gunther, Merchant, Governor of the Almshouse and Mayor of the City, and of James F. Wenman, Assistant-Engineer, President of the Cotton Exchange, and President of the Department of Parks.

From Sheldon's "Story of Volunteer Fire Department." Copyright, 1882, by Harper & Brothers.

"LET HER GO."

From Sheldon's "Story of Volunteer Fire Department.   Copyright, 1887, by Harper & Brothers.

FIREMEN'S MONUMENT, GREENWOOD CEMETERY.

° THE ° FIREMEN'S ° MONUMENT. °

N Greenwood Cemetery, far-famed city of the dead, there rises from the crest of Summit Hill a shaft of purest marble, surmounted by the figure of a Fireman in full uniform and in characteristic attitude.

On his strong left arm reposes the unconscious form of a little child which he has just rescued from a burning building. His right hand, outstretched and holding a trumpet reversed, directs his companions to new fields of effort in their tireless struggle with the raging conflagration, while his entire frame thrillingly expresses the tireless energy of the Volunteer.

This statue represents the *successful* strife of the New York Volunteer Firemen to save life and property menaced by the voracious element. But not always was this the result. Under the sod, beneath this heroic emblem, lie, awaiting the last trump, those members of the Department whose noble warfare with the flames terminated in the silence, but not the oblivion, of death. Above their mangled

288196

forms their mourning brother members have reared this monument to perpetuate the record of their daring deeds and the last act of self-sacrifice that sent them to untimely graves. Their names are inscribed on the mute yet eloquent stone, and their memory is tenderly cherished by those who shared their toils and dangers.

The lots upon which the memorial stands were purchased for the burial of Engineer George Kerr and Henry Fargis, Assistant Foreman of Southwark Engine Co-38, who were killed at the fire in Duane Street, New York, April 2d, 1848. The committee appointed by the Department to take charge of the erection of the monument consisted of the following gentlemen, all distinguished members of the Fire Department, viz.: Cornelius V. Anderson, George A. Buckingham, Lawrence Turnure, George W. Littell, John K. Bowen, Warren Bliven, James W. Barker, Furman Neefus, John A. Cregier and Charles McDougall.

The celebrated sculptor Robert E. Launitz was selected to design and build the monument and the result shows the wisdom of the choice. It would be difficult to conceive a more chaste and appropriate memento. The white marble shaft with its pedestal stands 23 feet 10 inches in hight. The statue is 4 feet 8 inches high. The shaft consists of three blocks on which are carved, in high relief, festoons of oak leaves—emblematic of strength and endurance. The pedestal is of symbolic design. The base block bears the Coat of arms of the City of New York; the pilasters are adorned with tastefully grouped hydrants, hose, hooks and ladders. Above the cornice is a cushion on which rest two Speaking Trumpets and a Fireman's Cap wreathed with oak leaves, to indicate the saving of a life by the wearer. Each corner of the cornice bears torches embellished with water lilies.

The railing surrounding the enclosure is of elaborate professional design. Hydrants surmounted by urns take the place of posts, while the gate is formed by hose pipes crossed by a hook, a ladder, a torch, an axe, a trumpet, and a "tormentor," bound together by the rope, and encircled by a wreath of laurel leaves. Over the gate is a scroll inscribed with the words "New York Fire Department, Incorporated A. D. 1798," and above the scroll is a bell.

Within the enclosure, which is 50 feet in diameter, there are 18 mounds placed in crescent form, singularly in harmony with Crescent Dell, which, with its embosomed lake, lies directly beneath the monument. It was not possible to secure the bodies of all the Firemen who lost their lives in the execution of their duty, owing to the fact that time had in many instances destroyed the identity of their burial places. The record that appears on the shaft is here given:

WILLIAM PETERSON	Foreman Engine Co. No. 15, May 19, 1811.
DAVID W. RAYMER	Engine Co. No. 40, March 8, 1827.
FRANCIS JOSEPH	Ass't Foreman Engine Co. No. 1, March 8, 1827.
CORNELIUS GARRISON	Engine Co. No. 32, July 5, 1832.
NATHANIEL BROWN	Engine Co. No. 42, September 25, 1832.
JAMES HEDGES	Engine Co. No. 12, September 25, 1832.
JOHN KNAPP	Engine Co. No. 32, March 6, 1834.
EUGENE UNDERHILL	Engine Co. No. 13, July 1, 1834.
FREDERICK WARD	Engine Co. No. 13, July 1, 1834.
RICHARD S. RITCHIE	Engine Co. No. 6, May 26, 1836.
THOMAS STORTON	Hose Co. No. 13, June 3, 1837.
JOHN BUCKLOH	Engine Co. No. 19, February 6, 1838.
JAMES S. WELLS	Engineer, April 15, 1840.
JAMES GLASGOW	Hose Co. No. 15, April 15, 1840.
AUGUSTUS COWDREY	Engine Co. No. 42, July 19, 1845.
GEORGE KERR	Engineer, April 2, 1848.
HENRY FARGIS	Ass't Foreman Engine Co. No. 38, April 2, 1848.
CHARLES J. DURANT	Hose Co. No. 35, April 2, 1848.
JOHN L. GUYRE	Engine Co. No. 14, April 24, 1850.
ARTHUR J. EVANS	Hose Co. No. 14, September 25, 1852.
GEORGE W. TRENCHARD	Hose Co. No. 16, June 2, 1853.
JOHN S. CARMAN	Engine Co. No. 5, October 30, 1853.
MICHAEL O'BRIEN	Hook and Ladder Co. No. 11, October 30, 1853.
ANDREW G. SCHENCK	Hook and Ladder Co. No. 1, April 25, 1854.
JOHN A. KEYSER	Hose Co. No. 8, April 25, 1854.
ALEXANDER MCKAY	Engine Co. No. 21, April 25, 1854.
DANIEL MCKAY	Engine Co. No. 21, April 25, 1854.
JAMES MCNULTY	Engine Co. No. 20, April 25, 1854.

The names of those killed between the years 1854 and the disbandment of the Department in 1865 have yet to be added to the above roll. The names also of the large number of Firemen whose families or friends preferred to bury them in their private plots, were not placed on the shaft.

The following is the dedicatory inscription :

"THE FIRE DEPARTMENT OF THE CITY OF NEW YORK HAVE CAUSED THIS MONUMENT TO BE ERECTED IN MEMORY OF THEIR COMPANIONS, WHO PERISHED IN DISCHARGE OF THEIR DUTY."
A. D. 1848.

The location of the monument is a fine one. It looks upon New York's un-rivalled bay and is very easy of access from the southern gate. Outside the enclosure, and flanking it, are individual memorial stones to Engineer Kerr and Ass't Foreman Fargis. Opposite, across the pathway, is the family plot of John L. Guyre, containing a handsome memorial. The beautiful and costly monument erected by Harry Howard, in memory of his foster mother, also faces it, while in the rear the stately column that lifts its urn-crowned head above all that is mor-tal of George Steers, the great ship-builder who built the yacht America and U. S. S. Niagara, tells a tale of mournful, unexpected death. Near by is the handsome tribute of the Excelsior Base Ball Club of Brooklyn to "Jim" Creighton, one of the first of the "lightning" pitchers, who was cut off suddenly in 1862 in the prime of his early manhood. The plot surrounding the Firemen's Monument is carefully tended and to-day summer flowers bloom above the graves and sweetly perfume the breeze which sadly sweeps through Greenwood's leafy shade.

⚬ VETERAN ⁎ FIREMEN'S ⁎ HOME. ⚬

N view of the active and faithful services of the Volunteer Firemen in the protection of life and property in the City of New York, it would seem to be unnecessary to state that disabled and superannuated members of the organization are entitled to the same sympathy and care that mark the treatment of those wards of the nation—the maimed and decrepit survivors of the wars of the Republic. Both these classes of men imperilled their health and lives in the interests of their fellows, and both suffer from their devotion to duty, in constitutions impaired by disease, or in the loss of limbs laid as a sacrifice upon the altar of the Commonwealth. Yet while the General Government has hastened to provide homes where the veteran soldier might find the protection due to his service to his country, no action has ever been taken by the municipality of New York, looking to the care of the worthy Veteran Volunteer Firemen, who in too many instances have been left to nurse, as best they might, the wounds and diseases incurred by their labors for the welfare of the City of their birth or adoption. This anomaly has been keenly felt for years by the Fireman and his friends, and projects, so far abortive, have been devised to enlist the aid of the authorities in establishing a Home for the deserving members of the force or to secure that praiseworthy object by private contributions. It

remained for Mr. George W. Anderson, President of the Veteran Firemen's Association, who had long had this matter at heart, to take a decisive step toward
the establishment of the institution in question. This gentleman has secured the
refusal of a desirable piece of property at Huguenot, on the south shore of Staten Island, a beautiful location fronting on Prince's Bay, and there is now every
hope that, with the cheerful co-operation of his fellow members, a suitable place
of refuge will shortly be provided for every meritorious Veteran and that the spectacle of a former member of the New York Volunteer Fire Department wandering
helpless through the streets of the great metropolis will no longer pain the gaze
of his sympathetic comrades. It may not be improper here to refer briefly to the
hardships endured by the Volunteer Firemen, in order to bring out in clear relief
the necessity and justice exhibited in founding the "Veteran Firemen's Home Association of the City of New York," under which title the institution for the
care of the Veterans is to be known. The trials and vicissitudes of the Veterans
are well known to and appreciated by the generation that knew them, but to
those citizens who have come upon the active scene of life since the disbandment of the Volunteer Department, the old system is little more than a tradition.

The motto of the Volunteer Firemen was "*Semper Paratus.*" They were *always*
on duty. Day and night, in Winter's storm or Summer's heat, they ever stood
ready for a call. Often and often did they turn into the bunks at the various
engine houses, too wearied to go to their homes after long hours spent in struggling
for the mastery of the fiery element, under such trying circumstances that it is
a marvel flesh and blood could stand it; and ere slumber could enfold their
tired frames, again would the brazen-tongued bell summon them to renewed efforts
with the dread destroyer. Drenched in Winter with spray from the hose or a
carelessly held pipe, or with rain that froze as it fell, or in Summer steaming with
the sweat brought out by the blazing sun or the caloric of the burning buildings,
poisoned with the fumes of deadly chemicals, is it a wonder that disease often
racked their frames and laid the foundation for permanent disability? No! must
be the emphatic answer from every candid person. The long and heavy drag of
the apparatuses was alone sufficient to exhaust the Firemen before the scene of
their labors was reached. They were frequently handicapped by deficient appurtenances; a disadvantage not readily appreciated by those whose ideas of the
service are formed entirely from the highly improved appliances of the present day.
In short, all the surrounding circumstances combined to make the life of the Vol-

unteer Fireman one of the severest in the whole sphere of human endeavor. There shall then, be no delay in the establishment of a Home where the disabled Veteran shall find the care and comfort his arduous and perilous duties have justly earned for him.

HOME FOR AGED AND INFIRM VOLUNTEER FIREMEN,
AT HUGUENOT, STATEN ISLAND, N. Y.

CHARTER · OF · THE
VETERAN FIREMEN'S HOME ASSOCIATION.

WE, THE UNDERSIGNED, GEORGE W. ANDERSON, JOHN MOLLER, BERNARD M. SWEENY, JAMES H. BARTLEY, JAMES F. WENMAN, FREDERICK A. RIDABOCK, EUGENE WARD, ABRAHAM SLAIGHT, ABRAM C. HULL, RICHARD EVANS, DANIEL GARVEY, THOMAS CLEARY, HENRY GUNTHER, WILLIAM ORFORD, THOMAS BARRETT, JOHN McCAULEY, PETER P. PULLIS, TIM- OTHY DONOVAN, ROBERT McWHINNEY, RICHARD H. NUGENT, GEORGE T. PATTERSON, WILLIAM H. BOYD, WILLIAM BRANDON, DANIEL D. CONOVER and HENRY JONES, all citizens of the State of New York, do hereby certify that we desire to form a society for the purpose hereinafter mentioned, in pursuance of the provisions of an Act of the Legislature of the State of New York, entitled "*An Act for the Incorporation of Societies or Clubs for certain lawful purposes,*" passed May 12th, 1875, and amendments thereto, and do hereby declare:

First. The name the said society is to be known by is "THE VETERAN FIREMEN'S HOME ASSOCIATION OF THE CITY OF NEW YORK."

Second. The particular nature and object for which the said Society is formed is to provide and maintain a Home for aged, infirm, invalid and indigent members of the late Volunteer Fire Department of the City of New York, so that those members of the late Volunteer Fire Department of the City of New York, who, by reason of adversity or force of circumstances, are, or become, so situated that they cannot, or shall not, be able to provide for themselves in their declining years, may be cared for, taken charge of, and their last days made comfortable by their former comrades in the dangers and risks of the duties incident to membership in the old Volunteer Fire Department of the City of New York. And further, for the mutual benefit of the members of this Association.

Third. The number of Directors or Managers of the said Society shall be seven, and the names of said Directors or Managers who are to manage the concerns of the Society for the first year are GEORGE W. ANDERSON, JOHN MOLLER, JAMES F. WENMAN, HENRY GUNTHER, GEORGE T. PATTERSON, DANIEL D. CONOVER and WILLIAM H. BOYD.

Fourth. The duration of said Society is to be for the term of fifty years.

IN WITNESS WHEREOF, we have hereunto affixed our hands and seals in the City of New York, on the twenty-seventh day of March, A.D., one thousand eight hundred and eighty-six.

GEORGE W. ANDERSON.	WILLIAM ORFORD.
JOHN MOLLER.	THOMAS BARRETT.
BERNARD M. SWEENY.	JOHN McCAULEY.
JAMES H. BARTLEY.	PETER P. PULLIS.
JAMES F. WENMAN.	TIMOTHY DONOVAN.
FREDERICK A. RIDABOCK.	ROBERT McWHINNEY.
EUGENE WARD.	RICHARD H. NUGENT.
ABRAHAM SLAIGHT.	G. T. PATTERSON.
ABRAM C. HULL.	WM. H. BOYD.
RICHARD EVANS.	WM. BRANDON.
DANIEL GARVEY.	D. D. CONOVER.
THOMAS CLEARY.	HENRY JONES.
HENRY GUNTHER.	

L. S.

STATE OF NEW YORK, CITY OF NEW YORK, } ss.
COUNTY OF NEW YORK.

On this twenty-seventh day of March, one thousand eight hundred and eighty-six, before me personally appeared, GEORGE W. ANDERSON, JOHN MOLLER, BERNARD M. SWEENY, JAMES H. BARTLEY, JAMES F. WENMAN. FREDERICK A. RIDABOCK, EUGENE WARD, ABRAHAM SLAIGHT, ABRAM C. HULL, RICHARD EVANS, DANIEL GARVEY, THOMAS CLEARY, HENRY GUNTHER, WILLIAM ORFORD, THOMAS BARRETT, JOHN McCAULEY, PETER P. PULLIS, TIMOTHY DONOVAN, ROBERT McWHINNEY, RICHARD H. NUGENT, GEORGE T. PATTERSON, WILLIAM H. BOYD, WILLIAM BRANDON, DANIEL D. CONOVER and HENRY JONES, known to me and to me known to be the individuals described in the foregoing certificate, and they severally before me signed the said certificate, and acknowledged that they signed the same, for the purposes therein mentioned.

L. S.

ALFRED T. ACKERT,
Notary Public, N. Y.

STATE OF NEW YORK, } ss.
CITY AND COUNTY OF NEW YORK.

I, GEORGE P. ANDREWS, one of the Justices of the Supreme Court in the First Judicial District of the State of New York, do hereby certify, that I have examined the Certificate of Incorporation of the Society designated as "THE VETERAN FIREMEN'S HOME ASSOCIATION OF THE CITY OF NEW YORK." and the right to establish or organize the same under the name and for the purposes therein mentioned, under and in pursuance of the Act entitled, "*An Act for the Incorporation of Societies or Clubs for certain lawful purposes*," passed May 12th, 1875, and amendments thereto, and the same meets my approbation and approval, and in accordance therewith I make this endorsement.

Dated, New York City, April 7th, 1886.

GEORGE P. ANDREWS.

STATE OF NEW YORK. } *ss.*
CITY AND COUNTY OF NEW YORK.

I, JAMES A. FLACK, Clerk of the said City and County, and Clerk of the Supreme Court of said State for said County, do certify that I have compared the preceding with the original Certificate of Incorporation of "THE VETERAN FIREMEN'S HOME ASSOCIATION OF THE CITY OF NEW YORK," on file in my office, and that the same is a correct transcript therefrom, and of the whole of such original.

Endorsed, filed and recorded 7th April, 1886.

IN WITNESS WHEREOF, I have hereunto subscribed my name and affixed my official seal this 8th day of May, 1886.

```
********
* SEAL. *
********
```

JAMES A. FLACK,
Clerk.

STATE OF NEW YORK. } *ss.*
OFFICE OF THE SECRETARY OF STATE.

I have compared the preceding with the original Certificate of Incorporation of "THE VETERAN FIREMEN'S HOME ASSOCIATION OF THE CITY OF NEW YORK," with acknowledgment thereto annexed, filed and recorded in this office on the ninth day of April, 1886, and do hereby certify the same to be a correct transcript therefrom, and of the whole of said original.

WITNESS my hand and the seal of office of the Secretary of State at the City of Albany, this ninth day of April, one thousand eight hundred and eighty-six.

```
********
* SEAL. *
********
```

FREDERICK COOK,
Secretary of State.

★ THE ★ SEVENTH ★ REGIMENT ★ BAND ★

ACCOMPANIES THE

VETERAN ★ FIREMEN'S ★ ASSOCIATION.

THIRTY years ago a stalwart Italian youth first beheld the Stars and Stripes floating from the mast-head of the U. S. Frigate "Congress" in the harbor of Genoa. The sight of the flag of the Great Republic filled him with a longing to reach the land which his Genoese compatriot, Columbus, had given to the world three and a half centuries before. That sturdy Italian boy, who had just turned his 21st year, was Carlo Cappa, the present Bandmaster of the leading regiment of the National Guard in the United States—the famous New York Seventh. Young Cappa was born in 1834, at Allessandria, in the Kingdom of Sardinia. His father was a Major of the 11th Infantry in the Sardinian Army, who followed the Eagles of the Great Napoleon in his campaign against Russia, was wounded

BANDMASTER CAPPA.

in the retreat from Moscow, and died when his son was only four years old. At ten, Carlo entered the Royal Academy of Asti, to which only the sons of soldiers are admitted, and remained five years, when he enlisted in the Band of the Sixth Lancers, and was present at the Battle of Novara in 1849. He remained in the army for six years, during four of which he was the first trombone of the band, when he enlisted in the U. S. Navy and made a two years' cruise in the Frigate "Congress," during the last six months of which he was leader of the band.

On the coming Birthday of Washington, Cappa will celebrate the 30th anniversary of his arrival in the promised land, February 22, 1858.   On his arrival he joined Ned Kendall's Band, and made a tour of the principal American cities, after which he became a member of Shelton's celebrated New York Band, of which Grafulla was leader, and when the latter became leader of the 7th Regiment Band in 1860 Cappa went with him, and remained until Grafulla's death.   Thus it will be seen that Cappa has served in the 7th Regiment Band for 25 years and been its leader since 1881, so when anybody asks the question: "What's the matter with Cappa?" the Seventh Regiment boys all chorus the answer in unison: "*Oh! he's all right.*"

In 1869 Cappa joined the Thomas Orchestra as first trombone, and remained with it for seven years; also played the euphonium with the Mapleson Opera for three years.   As Conductor of the Concerts in the Central Park, at Brighton Beach, Coney Island, and at the Louisville Exposition, Cappa has always given satisfaction to both the promoters and public, a fact which was signally illustrated in the latter case, since he was publicly complimented by the Board of Managers, decorated by the Festival Chorus, and elected Conductor for the following year by a large majority of the popular vote taken on the last days of the Exposition.

MISS HORTENSE PIERSE.

MISS HORTENSE PIERSE comes from that region so prolific of song birds—*the West.*   It would seem that the region which surprises the world with its energy, enterprise and wealth, is to be the source of our art inspiration.   Certainly some of our most gifted singers of both sexes have come to us from the West.   First, Abbott, then Nevada, and not least, if the last, Miss Pierse.

Miss Pierse is what is known in musical parlance as a dramatic Soprano, which will develop into the school of Parepa Rosa, Materna and Nilsson.   She has a full, sonorous and rich voice, of a strong individuality, reaching through three octaves, every note of which is perfect and available.   Voices of such range and power are exceedingly rare,

These gifts, combined with a queenly stateliness of person and beauty of face, make her a phenomenal artist. Miss Pierse began at an early age in Cincinnati, under Mr. Theodore Thomas, at the College of Music. She appeared in concerts in Cincinnati, Chicago and Cleveland. She has recently studied with the great teachers, Maretzek, Errani and Bristol. She is just out of her teens, of a commanding figure, a face, in its strong, beautiful character, almost tragic, and a blonde of the most pronounced style. She has mastered the chief parts in ten operas, together with the Oratorios of the "Messiah," "Creation," and others, and with her concert repertoire is probably the best equipped of the new school singers.

WALTER ROGERS, the wonderful young Cornet Soloist of Cappa's Band, was born at Delphi, Indiana, Oct. 14th, 1865. When about eight years old, his father, who is a thorough musician, commenced teaching him the violin, and his progress was very rapid. He had been playing the violin but a short time when he took up the cornet, intending it to be chiefly a pastime. But almost from the moment that he first touched the cornet he gave it a decided preference. In 1879, he entered the College of Music at Cincinnati, Ohio, and studied both instruments for about a year. During the next two years he played short engagements in different cities throughout his native State. At one of these engagements his cornet playing attracted the attention of Prof. Beissenberz, Musical Director at one of the theaters in Indianapolis. He at once offered Rogers a position in his orchestra, and the offer was accepted. The young Cornetist continued in this position for two years. In the Fall of 1884, Cappa's famous New York Seventh Regiment Band were engaged at the Louisville Exposition. With a generosity rarely shown, Mr. Beissenberz, though at a sacrifice to his own interests, took Rogers to Louisville and introduced him to Cappa. The famous leader was amazed at the wonderful abilities of so youthful a person and promised him an

WALTER ROGERS.

engagement the first vacancy that occurred.   The following Spring Cappa kept his promise by engaging Rogers as his Cornet Soloist at Brighton Beach and Central Park.   His career from that time has been one of continued success.   In Boston, Louisville, Quebec, and other places where he has appeared, he has won the highest praise for his matchless playing, and, brief as his career has been, he is already recognized as one of the greatest of Cornet Soloists.

MR. WILLIAM LACROIX, Trombone Soloist of the Seventh Regiment Band, was born in the city of New York, in the year 1860.   He comes from one of the greatest musical families in New York.   When, at the age of nine, his father saw what a liking he had for music, he taught him the French horn, afterwards placed him under Noll, Weingarten and Jacobi to study the violin, and afterwards became a member of Theodore Thomas' Orchestra, also of Damrosch's Orchestra. He studied harmony under W. G. Dietrich, and now holds the position of Chief de Orchestra under J. M. Lander of New York.   He is one of the finest musicians in New York, being a thorough performer upon the following instruments : Violin, double bass, tympan, trombone, baritone and tuba.   He is also president of the Dorsch Lodge, one of the largest musical societies in America

----

JOHN B. DAUSCH.

JOHN B. DAUSCH, the principal Oboi of the Seventh Regiment Band, was born in Landau, State of Bavaria, in 1846. He came to this country at the age of five years, studied harmony and piano under his father, and violin under F. Hermann, a pupil of Spohr, and oboi under Mr. Joseph Eller; was a member of Dr. Damrosch's Orchestra, and holds the position now as 1st oboi of the Peabody Institute of Baltimore, and also of the Philharmonic Society of the same city; was one of the 1st violins of Colonel Mapleson's Italian Opera Company under Signor Arditi's direction, and 1st oboi of the late Italian Opera Company

SIGNOR GIOAULIMO NORRITO.

SIGNOR GIOAULIMO NORRITO was born at Mazara del Vallo, Italy, at which place he received a first-class musical education. His father was a very distinguished musician and held in high esteem. He arrived in this country nine years ago, where he soon joined the orchestra of the Italian Opera, and two years later Cappa's Seventh Regiment Band as Piccolo Solo, which position he holds at present and is now performing before large audiences at Brighton Beach, Coney Island. He no doubt will make himself very popular with the people of the West who have a keen appreciation of a talented musician. His matchless performance upon the Piccolo has been the wonder of the musicians of the present day, and he now ranks as one of the foremost musicians in his line in the world.

JOHN DREWES.

MR. JOHN DREWES, the Clarinet Soloist of the Seventh Regiment Band, was born at Hanover, where he became the principal Clarinet in the king's private band. He came to America 25 years ago, where he at once became a member of the New York Philharmonic Society and holds the same position still. He also became a member of Theodore Thomas' Orchestra, a position he held for 15 years. At the same time he joined the Seventh Regiment Band under Mr. Grafulla, as his principal Clarinet, and still retains the same position under Mr. Cappa. Great offers have been made him to join other bands, but he could not be induced to leave Mr. Cappa.

CARL BEYER.

CARL BEYER was born in Erfurt, Germany, in 1849. From his 10th to 17th year he attended a German Government school, to study music under the best teachers. After being well educated he served in the German army for nine years, during which term he had to participate in the Franco German war. His regiment had then been designed to move to Hamburg. Mr. Beyer played in the principal orchestras and also took part in the great concert for the benefit of a National Stage conducted by Richard Wagner. This great master seemed to be delighted with military music also, for once, when the band played a serenade in his honor, he remarked that this kind of music had a great future, as more impressive than string music through the combination of brass with wind instruments; he called it a teacher of music to the people in general.

The Centennial year (1876) brought Mr. Beyer to America, where he took the conductorship of the "German Military Band," which made such immense success during their concert tour all over this country. His position did not satisfy him, however, any longer, and he left them to join the famous Seventh Regiment Band under the direction of Signor A. C. Cappa.

PROF. WITTGENSTEIN.

PROF. WITTGENSTEIN was born at Westphalia, Germany, in the year 1856, and is consequently now but thirty years of age. When he was but four years of age his parents left the Fatherland for America, having read and dreamed of the wonderful Arcadia beyond the sea and being desirous of testing its many boasted advantages for themselves. The elder Wittgenstein, the head of the family, was a merchant, and immediately upon arriving in Louisville—the family went directly there—went into business. He is now dead, but his widow still carries on the business. Out of a large family, Hugo was the only one who displayed any marked musical ability. When but four years of age, the aptitude for harmonious sounds began to display itself, and was manifested in a hundred various ways. It was his delight to linger at musical festivals, and he would follow strolling minstrels by the hour, imitating them in his childish way on corn-stalk flutes, old keys, and everything he could procure that would produce a sound.

Such a remarkable passion for music did not go unnoticed. Arrangements were made to place him under the tutorage of Prof. E. A. Bornshein, an accomplished musician of Louisville. He made rapid strides in his musical studies, and his proficiency in the use of the flute soon attracted local and then general attention. His services were in constant demand at private entertainments, and at ten years of age he was found filling an engagement in the old theater, which at that time stood on the corner of Fourth and Green Streets.

It was about this time that the Boston Quintette Club, then a famous organization, stopped at Louisville while on a professional tour to give an entertainment. The leader of the Quintette, Prof. Heindl, himself a renowned flutist, had his attention attracted to the precocious musician, and recognizing in him latent powers of more than ordinary capacity, made a proposition to Hugo's parents to take him to Boston and give him thorough instructions on the flute. The proposition was accepted, and after completing their tour the Club returned to Boston, taking with them young Hugo. Before departing, a farewell concert was given for the benefit of the boy musician, and it was quite a musical event for the city of Louisville.

After remaining in that city for five years, during which time he attained wonderful proficiency in the use of the flute, Hugo made a professional tour of the country, playing at the principal cities. Everywhere his superior musical talent was recognized, and he received very flattering notices from the Press.

In 1879 he accepted a position, under the famous Theodore Thomas, at the Cincinnati College of Music as first flutist in the orchestra and Professor of instruction in flute music. When Theodore Thomas retired from the directorship of the College Mr. Wittgenstein followed the fortunes of his leader and went to New York. So prominent at that time was his talent that a farewell concert was also given for his benefit in Cincinnati, in which some of the best musical talent of the company participated. After remaining in New York a while, the popular flutist identified himself with Mapleson's Italian Opera, with which organization he was connected for over five years, and since then has been connected with Sig. Cappa's Seventh Regiment Band.

Prof. Wittgenstein's flute playing is remarkable for its limpid sweetness and singular purity.   The tones he produces are clear, well sustained, and true to nature in their bird-like clearness, and in their execution betray a delicacy of expression that marks the presence of a master performer.   There is an indescribable something in his playing that appeals directly to the feelings of his audience, and therein consists, in a degree, his phenomenal success.

MR. WILLIAM GRIFFIN.

MR. WILLIAM GRIFFIN, Solo Cornetist of the 7th Regiment Band, was born in Ballincollig, County Cork, Ireland.   He enlisted in the British Army in the Royal Canadian Rifles in 1860 where he came under the tuition of Bandmaster Carey.   By hard practice and study he got to be the 1st Cornet player of his Band.   The Regiment was disbanded in 1869, when he volunteered into the 78th Highlanders, stationed at Halifax, N. S., where he came under Mr. McEleney, a very fine cornetist, brother-in-law to the great Dan Godfrey of the Grenadier Guards Band of London, England. The Regiment being ordered to England in 1871, he took his discharge and came to Boston and took part in the great Jubilee. Mr. M. Arbuckle specially engaged him to fill his position at the Globe Theater, under the leadership of Mr. Koppitz, while he (Arbuckle) was traveling with the Barnaby Concert party.   In 1873 Mr. Henry Tissington secured him as Soloist for Union Square Theater, New York, where since he has held the first position in all the principal orchestras.   In 1878 he joined Downing's 9th Regiment Band, and was also in the same Band under Arbuckle's direction, and remained with him until he died.   Then he became a member of Conterno's Band, playing at Brighton Beach, Coney Island.   In 1884 Mr. Cappa secured him for the 7th Regiment Band as his principal cornetist, which position he still holds.

A. H. W. BREMER.

$\mathcal{A}$LEXANDER HELGO WALDEMAR BREMER was born in Copenhagen, Denmark, in January, 1850.

The circumstance that Mr. Cremer's mother, before her marriage, was Lady's maid to Princess Charlotte, the mother of the present Queen of Denmark, procured him an early patroness in that high-born Lady, together with the offer to take charge of the boy's education as he grew up.

Having early evinced a love for music, young Alexander was permitted to choose it as his future field of action, and at nine years of age was given in charge of the best masters of the piano. His last Instructor on that instrument was Prof. Niels W. Gade, the Mendelssohn of Scandinavia. Thus at an early age, young Bremer became an accomplished player on the piano ; but the young musician evincing a strong desire for studying other instruments, his teachers advised the violin, which was reluctantly taken up, but soon laid aside as not congenial to the boy's tastes, which ran in the direction of a wind instrument. He now selected of his own choice the French Horn, or "Waldhorn" as it is generally called throughout Europe. Under the tuition of Prof. Wm. Schneider, a renowned Waldhorn player, rapid progress was made, and, at an early day, the young adept of that difficult instrument was called to perform before Her Royal Highness, the Princess Charlotte, and other members of the royal house. So favorable was the impression made by the young debutant on his select auditory, that from that time forth he became quite a favorite with the whole royal family, and was made an *elève* of the "Chapelle Royalle," being called upon twice every week to play at Court, accompanied by the Queen, a very fine musician and Pianist, on which instrument the royal Lady instructed all her own children. At this period of his career, the rare opportunity was afforded to young Bremer to play almost exclusively before crowned heads, having for his hearers or accompanists, the King and Queen of Denmark, Princess Alexandra, the present Princess of Wales, Princess Dagmar, now Empress of Russia, Princess Thyra, now Duchess of Cumberland, the Crown Prince, Frederick of Denmark, Prince George, now King of Greece, Prince Waldemar, and even the bethrothed of Princess Dagmar, Czar Alexander III. of this day. On one occasion, the young artist had the honor to play a duet with the present ruler of Russia, who is a fine performer on the Cornet-a-piston, but the spell of this position and its charming surroundings had to be broken at last, when the time arrived for young Bremer to see the outside world and to begin the battle of life on his own account.

At the parting from the country of his birth and from his earliest high-born protectors, the King presented Mr. Bremer with a beautiful Waldhorn, coupled with the gracious words : "At any time on your return to Denmark, the doors of our Court will be open to receive you."

Mr. Bremer came directly to the United States, landing at New York, which he has made his home. Under such circumstances, playing in Orchestras, under such leaders as Thomas, Damrosch, Arditi, Gilmore, and others, had to be resorted to, while Mr. Bremer's solo playing on the Waldhorn for a time had been confined to concerts, the only way in which Mr. Bremer has been able to make known the beauties and rare excellences of his chosen instrument.

The French Horn or Waldhorn descends from the old style hunting horns and is the most difficult of all the " Brasses." Very few, if any, amateurs are found playing the French Horn, since it requires not only a very delicate *embouchure* but persistent and patient daily practice. It has a soft, sentimental, sympathetic tone, far nobler than the cornet, and is the nearest approach among all wind instruments to the human voice ; especially adapted to interpret ballads and songs, which Mr. Bremer has made a specialty. It is more appropriate to indoor concert entertainments than any other brass instrument, by reason of its intrinsic quality of tone.

American audiences are accustomed to strong open air or grand orchestral effects, consequently, the delicately, long drawn out and refined tenderness of the French Horn is scarcely appreciated by them.

MISCELLANEOUS.

ALBERT WEBER, the great Pianomaker, who was one of New York's most celebrated characters and who died in 1879, was a Veteran Fireman and for many years an efficient member of Amity Hose Co. No. 38.

ALBERT WEBER.

A Veteran Fireman, and one of New York's most celebrated characters.

His portrait, which accompanies this article, shows at a glance that he was a man of great power and energy. He won his way to fame and fortune by those qualities which are pre-eminently characteristic of American enterprise and American business men.

A German, born in 1828, he came to this country in 1847. Being a skilled musician as well as a skilled pianomaker he soon found employment. His restless and energetic temperament, however, did not long permit him to remain in a subordinate capacity, and we find him, therefore, starting in business, though with a very limited capital, in Walker Street, to manufacture pianos.   He was the first of all the present great German Houses to start in the pianoforte trade, and commenced operations some months before his great rivals, Messrs. STEINWAY & SONS.   His success was almost instantaneous, and whatever the individual claims to public consideration of the various great American pianomakers, it was always conceded that ALBERT WEBER was the most popular of them all. This unique position he reached partly by the great merits of his instruments, partly by his tremendous "push," partly because the celebrated personages of the musical world found his pianofortes admirably adapted to accompany the voice, and for solo concert purposes, and partly because he was always foremost in his support of all worthy musical enterprises in this country and a "hale fellow well met" with everybody.

It can be said of ALBERT WEBER, without any exaggeration, that the great European singers and players built up his reputation almost without an effort on his part.   They discovered that the tone of his pianofortes possessed qualities not to be found in any other make of instrument, and they were not slow to express their appreciation of the fact.   Among the archives of the firm there is a collection of autograph letters that would be an acquisition to a museum.   They are the opinions of the artistic world on the merits of the Weber Piano, and the signatures of some of the world's most famous singers and musicians are among them, including the world-renowned *prima donnas,* NILSSON, LUCCA, PATTI, GERSTER, CARY, KELLOGG, VAN ZANDT, PAREPA-ROSA, ABBOTT, such other celebrities as CAMPANINI, GALASSI, ARDITI, MARIO, BERNHARDT, STRAKOSCH, SANTLEY, BRIGNOLI, CAPOUL, and the great Pianists, RIVE-KING, CARRENO, BOCK, RAVASZ and TOPP.

No other pianos were ever accorded such spontaneous and unequalled eulogy. It had been WEBER's good luck to discover a scale and a method of construction by which the tone—which, up to his time had been strong, powerful, and large in volume—gained that delicacy, softness, and especially that *sympathetic quality* which it had previously lacked.

This discovery, backed as it was by tremendous enterprise and incomparable energy, made WEBER's individual fortune.

When WEBER started in business, 40 years ago, he thought it a big thing to make one square piano a week.   At the time he died, in 1879, he turned out 50 pianos a week, principally concert grands and uprights, employed nearly a thousand men, owned two of the largest piano factories in the city, on 17th Street and

7th Avenue, magnificent warerooms on 5th Avenue, and had agencies in every city of any importance all over the country.

After his death he was succeeded in the business by his son, ALBERT, who, though barely out of his teens at the time, at once showed himself to be possessed of wonderful business capacity, tact and skill.

Young WEBER brought the business to even a greater state of prosperity, so that the firm turn out to-day 60 pianos a week on an average.

A few years ago a Branch House was opened in Chicago where the firm built a Music Hall, known as WEBER HALL, which is one of the finest in the country.

The year 1876 will be forever memorable for the great International Exhibition, held in Philadelphia. This Exhibition had a peculiar value and importance to all those concerned in those industries in which Americans had taken the lead during the past quarter of a century. It was the first time when juries, composed of the experts of the world, were called upon to decide not merely as to the relative merits of the different American manufactures, but as to the merits of the different claims of the various manufacturers to those inventions and improved methods of manufacture by which each particular American industry had reached its present condition of high development.

This was particularly true of the pianoforte business.

The Judges had not merely to determine the relative merits of the various makers of pianos ; they had to do more. They had to settle which of the makers was entitled to the proud distinction of having brought the American pianoforte to its present state of perfection, which has enabled it to take the lead among the Musical Instruments of the world.

After a prolonged, bitter and severe contest, in which all the leading manufacturers engaged, *the Centennial Judges Awarded the Highest Honors to the Weber Pianos.*

This put the climax to Weber's success, and from that time forth his position as the Head of the American Pianoforte Industry was scarcely even challenged. So much for the business career of this "Veteran Fireman."

Old ALBERT WEBER's personality as well as his social qualities were remarkable. He started as a workman in his shirt-sleeves and ended as one of the richest and most prominent men in New York, and as one of the most honored and popular members of the Lotos, Arcadian, and Manhattan Clubs.

He was equally at home in all positions, and even in the days of his greatest prosperity never forgot that he had once been a "Fireman," nor did he ever forget his old comrades of Hose No. 38.   This personality of WEBER's was so strong that when once started he went right to the front and staid there.

His struggles and trials, his memorable controversies with his competitors, his aggressiveness, his wit, humor, vitality, and absolutely indomitable pluck and spirit are all matters of New York history.   When WEBER found that he had an instrument which people liked, he set to work to place it before the public.   In this no man ever succeeded as he did.   He made friends right and left.   He even forced his enemies to say a kind word for him.   He strove, pushed and advertised with a persistence and energy that startled and appalled his competitors.   He rested neither by day nor by night.   He was everywhere and knew everybody.   He was a familiar feature at all "first nights" at the opera, at concerts, entertainments and meetings.   He seemed ubiquitous.   How he ever did it all remains a wonder to this day.

He was a master of the art of knowing how to handle the Press, had an unerring instinct for journalists of brains, and liberally rewarded the slightest favor. The newspaper men looked upon him as a friend and treated him as such.   They would do and did do more for ALBERT WEBER, with often no greater reward than a cigar or a kind word, than they would have done for many other houses for much money; for the newspaper men became interested in the little, dark, nervous man, with the twinkling black eyes, who treated them always so royally.

With artists and musicians he was an especial favorite, and the greatest of them were proud of his friendship.   He was an admirable entertainer, always had a fund of good stories, and was the very life of any party in which he might find himself.

He was a marvelous talker, and he talked with his eyes and his feet and his arms and his legs and his body as well as his tongue.

He gave himself out as a cynic, but was really one of the best-hearted men that ever lived.

He was one of New York's great men, was accepted and recognized as such, and when he died, New York, the piano trade and the whole musical world, felt that something had gone never to be replaced, and he was mourned for by many who had known, loved and admired him, but by none more sincerely than by his old comrades of Hose No. 38.

MAJOR J. B. POND,

THE POPULAR LECTURE AND MUSICAL MANAGER—A MAN WHO KNOWS NEARLY ALL THE DISTINGUISHED PERSONAGES WHO SPEAK THE ENGLISH LANGUAGE.

MAJOR J. B. POND, the well known manager of lecture and musical attractions, has had a varied and interesting career. He began life as a Printer's Devil in Fond-du-Lac, Wis., in 1854. In 1856 he went to Kansas and carried a Sharp's rifle (Beecher Bible) under John Brown. In 1857 he returned to Madison, Wis., and worked as a "jour." printer, and afterwards published a weekly paper in the northern part of the same State. Life did not go easy with him, but he met its vicissitudes with courage, good nature and tact, and realized all the advantages that it could produce in the limited field of his labors and duties. His military title is a genuine and not a bogus one. He gained it in the Third Wisconsin Cavalry, of which the late Ex-Governor William A. Barstow was Colonel and E. A. Calkins, now of Chicago, was Lieutenant-Colonel. He served with his regiment in the South-west and took an active part in the most stirring campaigns that occurred throughout that entire region. He was an excellent commanding officer, brave, full of resources, always ready for camp duty or for a fight, and was good to his men. He continued with a detachment of that regiment in service on the frontier till long after the last gun had been fired at the East, and was not mustered out until the Fall of 1865. He was formerly a Volunteer Fireman, in Water Witch Engine Co. No. 2, at Janesville, Wisconsin.

After the war Major Pond drifted to the far West, and engaged there and in other parts of the country in various business enterprises. But he did not find the work he was fitted for until he formed a connection with Redpath's Lecture Bureau, in Boston, of which he afterwards became proprietor. He subsequently disposed of that institution and became agent, manager and proprietor of the most popular and successful lecture and musical enterprises in the country. His especial pet and favorite was Henry Ward Beecher, with whom he was upon terms of the most intimate friendship, and whose praises he never wearies in reciting. Mr.

Beecher delivered 1,200 lectures under his auspices and they have traveled together 400,000 miles, never missing a train or an appointment. He had paid Mr. Beecher over $250,000 in money up to the time of his death. Clara Louise Kellogg's engagements were made by him during her most prosperous years. George W. Cable and Mark Twain lecture under his management, and he regards Mr. Cable as the first literary genius of the age. He took Talmage to England in 1879. This year the Rev. Dr. Joseph Parker, of City Temple, London, Mr. Charles Dickens, son of the great novelist, Max O'Rell, author of "John Bull and His Islands," and Mr. Archibald Forbes come to this country under his auspices. He has tried repeatedly to get Gladstone over here, not on a lecture tour exactly, but for something in that way, and would have succeeded had the g. o. m. been a dozen years younger. Wendell Phillips, John B. Gough and Ralph Waldo Emerson were under his management for many years previous to the close of their brilliant and useful lives. Major Pond probably knows more public and distinguished men, and is upon more intimate terms with them, than any other man living.

The beauty of Major Pond's character is that he has kept the simplicity of his manners and the youthful freshness of his heart through all this varied experience, in prosperity and adversity, when fortune smiled or misfortune frowned, at all times and under all circumstances. He has handled millions of money, has lived liberally and well, and is the friend of every man whom he ever knew. A printer with whom he was acquainted as a boy up in Wisconsin, thirty years ago, or a cavalry veteran who served under him in the war, is as welcome in his room at the Everett House in New York, as the Mayor of Chicago, or its most distinguished scholar or richest capitalist would be. He is 46 years old, is hale and robust, and has many years of active life still before him.

HENRY S. BILLINGS.

HENRY S. BILLINGS was born at Waterford, Maine, June 10th, 1833; entered service of Erie and Atlantic Sleeping Coach Co., April 5th, 1865, as conductor; promoted to Assistant Superintendent January 1st, 1867, to Superintendent July 19th, 1871; above company merged into P. P. C. Co. June 1st, 1872; continues in the service of Pullman's Palace Car Co. as Division Superintendent to date.

DESCRIPTIVE PROGRAMME OF RECEPTION AND GRAND CONCERT,

UNDER THE AUSPICES OF THE

VETERAN FIREMEN'S ASSOCIATION OF THE CITY OF NEW YORK,

By Cappa's Seventh Regiment Band, N. G. S. N. Y.

And the Young and Talented Soprano, MISS HORTENSE PIERSE, on their Transcontinental Excursion,
September, 1887,

Stopping at CHICAGO, OMAHA, SALT LAKE CITY, SACRAMENTO, SAN FRANCISCO, DENVER, KANSAS CITY, LOUISVILLE,
CINCINNATI AND CLEVELAND.

1. OVERTURE—William Tell, ... *Rossini*
   CAPPA'S SEVENTH REGIMENT BAND.

   No Overture has ever been rendered by a Military Band that has received greater favor. It is considered by leaders as one of the most effective productions of its class, and is an ever welcome feature on the programme of a Musical Festival, and never fails to make a deep impression. Mr. Cappa had the opportunity of being present in Asti, Italy, and witnessing its production under the conductorship of the composer, and while this rendition may appear to the listener different from the former versions, it is a faithful interpretation of the work.

2. CORNET SOLO—Air Varie, ... *Rogers*
   MR. WALTER ROGERS.

   There has been no greater progress in the musical world the past twenty years than that of surmounting the difficulties of the favorite of instruments, the Cornet, and no one has more fully proved to be its master than the young American, Mr. Rogers. Brief as his career has been, he is already recognized as one of the greatest Cornet Soloists.

3. GRAND SELECTION—Lucia di Lammermoor, ... *Donizetti*
   Containing all the gems of Donizetti's Masterpiece and concluding with the famous Sextette.
   CAPPA'S SEVENTH REGIMENT BAND.

4. VALSE DE JULIET, ... *Gounod-Raff*
   MR. ADOLPH GLOSE.

   Mr. Glose is foremost among the popular Pianists of the day. He has been Solo Pianist with Miss Clara Kellogg three seasons. Wherever he has appeared there has been but one expression, and that "the surprise of the evening."

5. INFLAMMATUS—Stabat Mater, ... *Rossini*
   MISS HORTENSE PIERSE AND SEVENTH REGIMENT BAND.

   Miss Pierse is what is known in musical parlance as a *Dramatic Soprano*, the school of Parepa Rosa, Materna and Nilsson. She has a full, sonorous and rich voice of strong individuality, reaching through three octaves, every note of which is perfect and available. These gifts, combined with queenly stateliness and beauty of face, make her a phenomenal artist, and capable of rendering the Inflammatus to absolute perfection.

6. HUNGARIAN RHAPSODIE—No. 2. . . . . *Liszt*

   Foremost in its difficulties for a Military Band stands the above Rhapsodie, the test piece for all the greatest Pianists. The marvelous performer Josefy expressed his utter astonishment at hearing it played at a Band Concert. The classical ear finds in this wonderful music-production a rich feast, while the public generally can see and hear that there is something extraordinary going on when the band have once got fairly into it. It is a masterpiece, and its performance by Cappa's Band has won the highest eucomiums ever paid a similar organization.

7. PATROL – General Boulanger's En revenant de la Revue,   .   .   . *G. Wiegand*

SYNOPSIS—Represents the Band of the Brigade Coming in Distance.—The Gradual Approach.—The Passing by the General Boulanger.—And the Gradual Passing Away in the Distance.—Introducing La Marseillaise.

This is the new popular French national air, which was recently published in the New York *Herald* and which was produced for the first time in America by Cappa's Band.

8. ARIA, Scene and Duet Finale—Trovatore,   .   .   .   *Verdi*

FOR CORNET AND TROMBONE.

MR. W. GRIFFIN.   MR. W. LACROIX.

No Opera has been composed that for melody, tunefulness and rapturous harmony can be compared with the classical and popular musical creation of "Il Trovatore." It is given under the most elaborate auspices from Orchestra and Chorus, the scenic representations down to the whistling street boy and hand organ, being unsurpassed and possessing a charm that exceeds that of any other Opera. One of the latest and most telling effects is this Duet produced by the Cornet and Trombone, accompanied by the full Military Band, the "Miserere" played by the supplementary band in the distance.

9. THE NIGHTINGALE, ...   *Delibes*

MISS HORTENSE PIERSE.

Of this young artist the *Brooklyn Eagle* says: "In the programme of the Amphion Society, the third number was a solo by Miss Hortense Pierse, a tall and striking blonde, who sang 'The Nightingale,' by Delibes, which was loudly applauded. Her rich voice gives evidence of careful training, and her rendering of the song was pleasing and graceful. Her second number was encored and repeated. Afterwards Miss Pierse gave two short songs, 'Once Again,' by Lassen, and 'Swedish Air,' by Peruzzi, in an artistic manner."

10. PIANO SOLO—Pasquinade, ...   *Gottschalk*

MR. ADOLF GLOSE.

"Mr. Glose in a Pasquinade exhibited a marvelous command over the Piano. One could imagine almost that he made the instrument speak. His touch is exquisite, and his runs are remarkable for their smoothness and brilliancy."—*N. Y. Tribune.*

11. REMINISCENCES OF THE VETERAN FIREMEN,   .   .   .   *Cappa*

DEDICATED TO MR. GEORGE W. ANDERSON, PRESIDENT OF THE VETERAN
FIREMEN'S ASSOCIATION OF THE CITY OF NEW YORK.

Introducing conversation of the Firemen in the Engine House; Fire Alarm; The Start; Running to the Fire; The Falling of the Wall and Grand Finale. Mr. Anderson used to run with Phœnix Hose No. 22, of which he was foreman for many years. He was a gallant fireman, and after the decline of the Volunteer Fire Department of New York, he kept on growing in usefulness, until he is now one of the most highly esteemed citizens of the metropolis, and although having amassed a fortune and able to retire and live in luxury, he remains "one of the boys," and is not the last to render material aid to almost every deserving charity, especially where a Volunteer Fireman or his family is the object.

12. GRAND FANTASIE—Introducing melodies from England, Scotland and Ireland,   *Baetens*

Although Mr. Cappa is a son of Italy, he is gifted with a touch of nature that finds its way to all hearts. He realizes that America's great cosmopolitans will never lose their fondness for the familiar melodies of their native land. Wherever his famous organization appears, the audiences frequently interrupt this performance with rounds of applause and deafening cheers.

THE sincere thanks of the compiler of this small book are herewith tendered to Messrs. Harper Bros. for the use of plates from Sheldon's "Story of Volunteer Fire Department," to Mr. James F. Wenman for the article on the Veteran Firemen's Association, and to Mr. James Cameron, Secretary of the Firemen's Ball Committee, for the brief history of said Committee.